<u>Super Ha</u>

Phone Nur

Calendar Dates

Weekly Planner

<u>Bonuses</u>

Website Passwords Log

Personal Goals

Vacation Planning

Packing List

Party Planning

Christmas Day Planner

Grocery List

<u>Notebook</u>

Lined Pages

Notes

Grid Dots

Gift ideas with a personal touch

CustomNameGifts.com

Follow Us On Instagram

@MariaLeonaDesign

Important Info

FAMILY NAME: ....

ADDRESS: ....

HOME PHONE: ....

IN AN EMERGENCY CALL:

PARENT 1

NAME: ....

WORK PHONE: ....

CELL PHONE: ....

PARENT 2

NAME: ....

WORK PHONE: ....

CELL PHONE: ....

CHILDREN'S NAMES

....

....

....

....

CHILDREN'S CELL PHONE NUMBERS

....

....

....

....

SCHOOL NAME(S)

....

....

....

....

SCHOOL PHONE NUMBERS

....

....

....

....

EXTENDED FAMILY

....

....

....

....

NEIGHBORS & FRIENDS

....

....

....

....

NOTES:

Phone Numbers - eMails

MILY	FRIENDS
EQUENT PLAYDATES	NEIGHBORS
ABYSITTERS	SCHOOLS/DAYCARE
IDS' AFTER-SCHOOL PROGRAMS	KIDS' FAVORITE ATTRACTIONS
ALONS	GYMS/CLUBS
RESTAURANTS	TAKE-OUT/DELIVERY
VET	GROOMER

Phone Numbers - eMails

CONTRACTORS

_____
_____
_____
_____

HANDYMAN

_____
_____
_____
_____

REPAIRS

_____
_____
_____
_____

CLEANING SERVICES

_____
_____
_____
_____

LAWN SERVICE

_____
_____
_____
_____

SNOW REMOVAL

_____
_____
_____
_____

GARBAGE PICKUP

_____
_____
_____
_____

RECYCLING PICKUP

_____
_____
_____
_____

DECORATOR

_____
_____
_____

OTHER

_____
_____
_____

NOTES:

Phone Numbers - eMails

NTRACTORS

HANDYMAN

PAIRS

CLEANING SERVICES

WN SERVICE

SNOW REMOVAL

ARBAGE PICKUP

RECYCLING PICKUP

ECORATOR

OTHER

NOTES:

January

Monthly Focus

1 _____
2 _____
3 _____

Special Dates

_____ _____
_____ _____
_____ _____
_____ _____
_____ _____

Home Keeping Tasks

☐ _____
☐ _____
☐ _____
☐ _____
☐ _____
☐ _____
☐ _____

Goals for the Month

_____ ☐
_____ ☐
_____ ☐
_____ ☐
_____ ☐
_____ ☐

_____ ☐
_____ ☐
_____ ☐
_____ ☐
_____ ☐
_____ ☐

_____ ☐
_____ ☐
_____ ☐
_____ ☐
_____ ☐
_____ ☐

Notes

February

Monthly Focus

Top Three Things

1 _____
2 _____
3 _____

Special Dates

_____
_____
_____
_____
_____

Home Keeping Tasks

☐ _____
☐ _____
☐ _____
☐ _____
☐ _____
☐ _____
☐ _____

Goals for the Month

☐ _____
☐ _____
☐ _____
☐ _____
☐ _____
☐ _____

☐ _____
☐ _____
☐ _____
☐ _____
☐ _____
☐ _____

☐ _____
☐ _____
☐ _____
☐ _____
☐ _____
☐ _____

Notes
_____
_____
_____
_____
_____
_____
_____
_____
_____
_____
_____
_____
_____
_____
_____
_____
_____
_____
_____
_____
_____
_____
_____

March

Monthly Focus

Top Three Things

1 _____
2 _____
3 _____

Special Dates

___ _____
___ _____
___ _____
___ _____
___ _____

Home Keeping Tasks

☐ _____
☐ _____
☐ _____
☐ _____
☐ _____
☐ _____
☐ _____

Goals for the Month

_____ ☐
_____ ☐
_____ ☐
_____ ☐
_____ ☐
_____ ☐

_____ ☐
_____ ☐
_____ ☐
_____ ☐
_____ ☐
_____ ☐

_____ ☐
_____ ☐
_____ ☐
_____ ☐
_____ ☐
_____ ☐

Notes

April

nthly Focus

Top Three Things

1 _____
2 _____
3 _____

Special Dates

_____
_____
_____
_____

als for the Month

Home Keeping Tasks

☐ _____
☐ _____
☐ _____
☐ _____
☐ _____
☐ _____
☐ _____

☐
☐
☐
☐
☐
☐

☐
☐
☐
☐
☐
☐

☐
☐
☐
☐
☐
☐

Notes
_____
_____
_____
_____
_____
_____
_____
_____
_____
_____
_____
_____
_____
_____
_____
_____
_____
_____
_____
_____
_____
_____
_____

May

Monthly Focus

Top Three Things

1 _____
2 _____
3 _____

Special Dates

_____ _____
_____ _____
_____ _____
_____ _____
_____ _____

Home Keeping Tasks

☐ _____
☐ _____
☐ _____
☐ _____
☐ _____
☐ _____
☐ _____

Goals for the Month

_____ ☐
_____ ☐
_____ ☐
_____ ☐
_____ ☐
_____ ☐

_____ ☐
_____ ☐
_____ ☐
_____ ☐
_____ ☐
_____ ☐

_____ ☐
_____ ☐
_____ ☐
_____ ☐
_____ ☐
_____ ☐

Notes

_____
_____
_____
_____
_____
_____
_____
_____
_____
_____
_____
_____
_____
_____
_____
_____
_____
_____
_____
_____
_____
_____

June

Monthly Focus

Top Three Things

1 _____
2 _____
3 _____

Special Dates

_____
_____
_____
_____

Home Keeping Tasks

☐ _____
☐ _____
☐ _____
☐ _____
☐ _____
☐ _____
☐ _____

Goals for the Month

_____ ☐
_____ ☐
_____ ☐
_____ ☐
_____ ☐
_____ ☐

_____ ☐
_____ ☐
_____ ☐
_____ ☐
_____ ☐
_____ ☐

_____ ☐
_____ ☐
_____ ☐
_____ ☐
_____ ☐
_____ ☐

Notes

July

Monthly Focus

Top Three Things

1 _____
2 _____
3 _____

Special Dates

_____ _____
_____ _____
_____ _____
_____ _____
_____ _____

Home Keeping Tasks

☐ _____
☐ _____
☐ _____
☐ _____
☐ _____
☐ _____
☐ _____

Goals for the Month

☐
☐
☐
☐
☐
☐

☐
☐
☐
☐
☐
☐

☐
☐
☐
☐
☐

Notes

August

nthly Focus

Top Three Things

1 _____
2 _____
3 _____

Special Dates

_____
_____
_____
_____
_____

Home Keeping Tasks

☐ _____
☐ _____
☐ _____
☐ _____
☐ _____
☐ _____
☐ _____

als for the Month

_____ ☐
_____ ☐
_____ ☐
_____ ☐
_____ ☐
_____ ☐

_____ ☐
_____ ☐
_____ ☐
_____ ☐
_____ ☐
_____ ☐

_____ ☐
_____ ☐
_____ ☐
_____ ☐
_____ ☐
_____ ☐

Notes

_____
_____
_____
_____
_____
_____
_____
_____
_____
_____
_____
_____
_____
_____
_____
_____
_____
_____
_____
_____
_____
_____
_____
_____
_____
_____
_____

September

Monthly Focus

Top Three Things

1 _____
2 _____
3 _____

Special Dates

_____ _____
_____ _____
_____ _____
_____ _____
_____ _____

Home Keeping Tasks

- ☐ _____
- ☐ _____
- ☐ _____
- ☐ _____
- ☐ _____
- ☐ _____
- ☐ _____

Goals for the Month

- ☐ _____
- ☐ _____
- ☐ _____
- ☐ _____
- ☐ _____
- ☐ _____

- ☐ _____
- ☐ _____
- ☐ _____
- ☐ _____
- ☐ _____
- ☐ _____

- ☐ _____
- ☐ _____
- ☐ _____
- ☐ _____
- ☐ _____
- ☐ _____

Notes

_____
_____
_____
_____
_____
_____
_____
_____
_____
_____
_____
_____
_____
_____
_____
_____
_____
_____
_____
_____
_____

October

nthly Focus

Top Three Things

1 _____
2 _____
3 _____

Special Dates

_____
_____
_____
_____
_____

Home Keeping Tasks

☐ _____
☐ _____
☐ _____
☐ _____
☐ _____
☐ _____
☐ _____

als for the Month

☐ _____
☐ _____
☐ _____
☐ _____
☐ _____
☐ _____

☐ _____
☐ _____
☐ _____
☐ _____
☐ _____
☐ _____

☐ _____
☐ _____
☐ _____
☐ _____
☐ _____
☐ _____

Notes

_____
_____
_____
_____
_____
_____
_____
_____
_____
_____
_____
_____
_____
_____
_____
_____
_____
_____
_____
_____
_____
_____
_____
_____
_____

November

Monthly Focus

Top Three Things

1 _____
2 _____
3 _____

Special Dates

_____ _____
_____ _____
_____ _____
_____ _____
_____ _____

Home Keeping Tasks

☐ _____
☐ _____
☐ _____
☐ _____
☐ _____
☐ _____
☐ _____

Goals for the Month

_____ ☐
_____ ☐
_____ ☐
_____ ☐
_____ ☐
_____ ☐

_____ ☐
_____ ☐
_____ ☐
_____ ☐
_____ ☐
_____ ☐

_____ ☐
_____ ☐
_____ ☐
_____ ☐
_____ ☐
_____ ☐

Notes

December

Monthly Focus

Top Three Things

1 _____
2 _____
3 _____

Special Dates

Home Keeping Tasks

☐ _____
☐ _____
☐ _____
☐ _____
☐ _____
☐ _____
☐ _____

Goals for the Month

☐
☐
☐
☐
☐
☐

☐
☐
☐
☐
☐
☐

☐
☐
☐
☐
☐
☐

Notes

Week 1

Monday

Tuesday

Wednesday

Thursday

Friday

Saturday

Sunday

Places to Go

- ○
- ○
- ○
- ○
- ○
- ○

People to See

- ○
- ○
- ○
- ○
- ○
- ○

Things to Do

- ○
- ○
- ○
- ○
- ○
- ○
- ○
- ○
- ○
- ○
- ○
- ○
- ○

Special Reminders

- ○
- ○
- ○
- ○
- ○
- ○

Week 2

nday

esday

ednesday

hursday

riday

Saturday

Sunday

Places to Go
- ○
- ○
- ○
- ○
- ○
- ○

People to See
- ○
- ○
- ○
- ○
- ○
- ○

Things to Do
- ○
- ○
- ○
- ○
- ○
- ○
- ○
- ○
- ○
- ○
- ○
- ○
- ○

Special Reminders
- ○
- ○
- ○
- ○
- ○
- ○
- ○

Week 3

Monday

Tuesday

Wednesday

Thursday

Friday

Saturday

Sunday

Places to Go

People to See

Things to Do

Special Reminders

Week 4

nday

esday

ednesday

hursday

riday

Saturday

Sunday

Places to Go

- ○
- ○
- ○
- ○
- ○
- ○

People to See

- ○
- ○
- ○
- ○
- ○
- ○

Things to Do

- ○
- ○
- ○
- ○
- ○
- ○
- ○
- ○
- ○
- ○
- ○
- ○
- ○

Special Reminders

- ○
- ○
- ○
- ○
- ○
- ○

Week 5

Monday

Tuesday

Wednesday

Thursday

Friday

Saturday

Sunday

Places to Go

People to See

Things to Do

Special Reminders

Week 6

nday

esday

ednesday

hursday

riday

Saturday

Sunday

Places to Go

- ○
- ○
- ○
- ○
- ○
- ○

People to See

- ○
- ○
- ○
- ○
- ○
- ○

Things to Do

- ○
- ○
- ○
- ○
- ○
- ○
- ○
- ○
- ○
- ○
- ○
- ○

Special Reminders

- ○
- ○
- ○
- ○
- ○
- ○
- ○

Week 7

Monday

Tuesday

Wednesday

Thursday

Friday

Saturday

Sunday

Places to Go

-
-
-
-
-
-
-

People to See

-
-
-
-
-
-

Things to Do

-
-
-
-
-
-
-
-
-
-
-
-
-

Special Reminders

-
-
-
-
-
-
-

Week 8

nday

esday

ednesday

hursday

riday

Saturday

Sunday

Places to Go

- ○
- ○
- ○
- ○
- ○
- ○

People to See

- ○
- ○
- ○
- ○
- ○
- ○

Things to Do

- ○
- ○
- ○
- ○
- ○
- ○
- ○
- ○
- ○
- ○
- ○
- ○

Special Reminders

- ○
- ○
- ○
- ○
- ○
- ○
- ○

Week 8

Monday

Tuesday

Wednesday

Thursday

Friday

Saturday

Sunday

Places to Go

People to See

Things to Do

Special Reminders

Week 9

nday

esday

ednesday

nursday

riday

Saturday

Sunday

Places to Go

○ ....
○ ....
○ ....
○ ....
○ ....
○ ....

People to See

○ ....
○ ....
○ ....
○ ....
○ ....
○ ....

Things to Do

○ ....
○ ....
○ ....
○ ....
○ ....
○ ....
○ ....
○ ....
○ ....
○ ....
○ ....
○ ....

Special Reminders

○ ....
○ ....
○ ....
○ ....
○ ....
○ ....
○ ....

Week 10

Monday

Tuesday

Wednesday

Thursday

Friday

Saturday

Sunday

Places to Go

People to See

Things to Do

Special Reminders

Week 11

nday

esday

ednesday

hursday

riday

Saturday

Sunday

Places to Go

○
○
○
○
○
○

People to See

○
○
○
○
○
○

Things to Do

○
○
○
○
○
○
○
○
○
○
○
○
○

Special Reminders

○
○
○
○
○
○
○

Week 12

Monday

Tuesday

Wednesday

Thursday

Friday

Saturday

Sunday

Places to Go

People to See

Things to Do

Special Reminders

Week 13

nday

esday

ednesday

hursday

riday

Saturday

Sunday

Places to Go

○
○
○
○
○
○

People to See

○
○
○
○
○
○

Things to Do

○
○
○
○
○
○
○
○
○
○
○
○
○

Special Reminders

○
○
○
○
○
○
○

Week 14

Monday

Tuesday

Wednesday

Thursday

Friday

Saturday

Sunday

Places to Go

- ○
- ○
- ○
- ○
- ○
- ○

People to See

- ○
- ○
- ○
- ○
- ○
- ○

Things to Do

- ○
- ○
- ○
- ○
- ○
- ○
- ○
- ○
- ○
- ○
- ○
- ○

Special Reminders

- ○
- ○
- ○
- ○
- ○
- ○
- ○

Week 15

nday

esday

ednesday

nursday

riday

Saturday

Sunday

Places to Go
- ○
- ○
- ○
- ○
- ○
- ○

People to See
- ○
- ○
- ○
- ○
- ○
- ○

Things to Do
- ○
- ○
- ○
- ○
- ○
- ○
- ○
- ○
- ○
- ○
- ○
- ○

Special Reminders
- ○
- ○
- ○
- ○
- ○
- ○
- ○

Week 16

Monday

Tuesday

Wednesday

Thursday

Friday

Saturday

Sunday

Places to Go

- ○
- ○
- ○
- ○
- ○
- ○

People to See

- ○
- ○
- ○
- ○
- ○
- ○

Things to Do

- ○
- ○
- ○
- ○
- ○
- ○
- ○
- ○
- ○
- ○
- ○
- ○

Special Reminders

- ○
- ○
- ○
- ○
- ○
- ○
- ○

Week 17

nday

esday

ednesday

hursday

riday

Saturday

Sunday

Places to Go

- ○
- ○
- ○
- ○
- ○
- ○

People to See

- ○
- ○
- ○
- ○
- ○
- ○

Things to Do

- ○
- ○
- ○
- ○
- ○
- ○
- ○
- ○
- ○
- ○
- ○
- ○

Special Reminders

- ○
- ○
- ○
- ○
- ○
- ○
- ○

Week 18

Monday

Tuesday

Wednesday

Thursday

Friday

Saturday

Sunday

Places to Go

- ◯
- ◯
- ◯
- ◯
- ◯
- ◯

People to See

- ◯
- ◯
- ◯
- ◯
- ◯
- ◯

Things to Do

- ◯
- ◯
- ◯
- ◯
- ◯
- ◯
- ◯
- ◯
- ◯
- ◯
- ◯
- ◯
- ◯

Special Reminders

- ◯
- ◯
- ◯
- ◯
- ◯
- ◯
- ◯

Week 19

nday

esday

ednesday

hursday

riday

Saturday

Sunday

Places to Go

○
○
○
○
○
○

People to See

○
○
○
○
○
○

Things to Do

○
○
○
○
○
○
○
○
○
○
○
○

Special Reminders

○
○
○
○
○
○
○

Week 20

Monday

Tuesday

Wednesday

Thursday

Friday

Saturday

Sunday

Places to Go

- ○
- ○
- ○
- ○
- ○
- ○

People to See

- ○
- ○
- ○
- ○
- ○
- ○

Things to Do

- ○
- ○
- ○
- ○
- ○
- ○
- ○
- ○
- ○
- ○
- ○
- ○
- ○
- ○

Special Reminders

- ○
- ○
- ○
- ○
- ○
- ○
- ○

Week 21

nday

esday

ednesday

hursday

riday

Saturday

Sunday

Places to Go

○
○
○
○
○
○

People to See

○
○
○
○
○
○

Things to Do

○
○
○
○
○
○
○
○
○
○
○
○
○

Special Reminders

○
○
○
○
○
○
○

Week 22

Monday

Tuesday

Wednesday

Thursday

Friday

Saturday

Sunday

Places to Go

-
-
-
-
-
-

People to See

-
-
-
-
-
-

Things to Do

-
-
-
-
-
-
-
-
-
-
-
-
-

Special Reminders

-
-
-
-
-
-

Week 23

Monday

Tuesday

Wednesday

Thursday

Friday

Saturday

Sunday

Places to Go

- ◯
- ◯
- ◯
- ◯
- ◯
- ◯

People to See

- ◯
- ◯
- ◯
- ◯
- ◯
- ◯

Things to Do

- ◯
- ◯
- ◯
- ◯
- ◯
- ◯
- ◯
- ◯
- ◯
- ◯
- ◯
- ◯
- ◯

Special Reminders

- ◯
- ◯
- ◯
- ◯
- ◯
- ◯
- ◯

Week 24

Monday

Tuesday

Wednesday

Thursday

Friday

Saturday

Sunday

Places to Go

- ○
- ○
- ○
- ○
- ○
- ○

People to See

- ○
- ○
- ○
- ○
- ○
- ○

Things to Do

- ○
- ○
- ○
- ○
- ○
- ○
- ○
- ○
- ○
- ○
- ○
- ○

Special Reminders

- ○
- ○
- ○
- ○
- ○
- ○
- ○

Week 25

nday

esday

ednesday

hursday

riday

Saturday

Sunday

Places to Go

- ◯
- ◯
- ◯
- ◯
- ◯
- ◯

People to See

- ◯
- ◯
- ◯
- ◯
- ◯
- ◯

Things to Do

- ◯
- ◯
- ◯
- ◯
- ◯
- ◯
- ◯
- ◯
- ◯
- ◯
- ◯
- ◯
- ◯

Special Reminders

- ◯
- ◯
- ◯
- ◯
- ◯
- ◯
- ◯

Week 26

Monday

Tuesday

Wednesday

Thursday

Friday

Saturday

Sunday

Places to Go

- ◯
- ◯
- ◯
- ◯
- ◯
- ◯

People to See

- ◯
- ◯
- ◯
- ◯
- ◯
- ◯

Things to Do

- ◯
- ◯
- ◯
- ◯
- ◯
- ◯
- ◯
- ◯
- ◯
- ◯
- ◯
- ◯

Special Reminders

- ◯
- ◯
- ◯
- ◯
- ◯
- ◯
- ◯

Week 27

nday

esday

ednesday

hursday

riday

Saturday

Sunday

Places to Go

- ○
- ○
- ○
- ○
- ○
- ○

People to See

- ○
- ○
- ○
- ○
- ○
- ○

Things to Do

- ○
- ○
- ○
- ○
- ○
- ○
- ○
- ○
- ○
- ○
- ○
- ○

Special Reminders

- ○
- ○
- ○
- ○
- ○
- ○
- ○

Week 28

Monday

Tuesday

Wednesday

Thursday

Friday

Saturday

Sunday

Places to Go

- ○
- ○
- ○
- ○
- ○
- ○

People to See

- ○
- ○
- ○
- ○
- ○
- ○

Things to Do

- ○
- ○
- ○
- ○
- ○
- ○
- ○
- ○
- ○
- ○
- ○
- ○
- ○

Special Reminders

- ○
- ○
- ○
- ○
- ○
- ○
- ○

Week 29

nday

esday

ednesday

hursday

riday

Saturday

Sunday

Places to Go

○
○
○
○
○
○

People to See

○
○
○
○
○
○

Things to Do

○
○
○
○
○
○
○
○
○
○
○
○
○

Special Reminders

○
○
○
○
○
○
○

Week 30

Monday

Tuesday

Wednesday

Thursday

Friday

Saturday

Sunday

Places to Go

People to See

Things to Do

Special Reminders

Week 31

nday

esday

ednesday

hursday

riday

Saturday

Sunday

Places to Go

○ ....
○ ....
○ ....
○ ....
○ ....
○ ....

People to See

○ ....
○ ....
○ ....
○ ....
○ ....
○ ....

Things to Do

○ ....
○ ....
○ ....
○ ....
○ ....
○ ....
○ ....
○ ....
○ ....
○ ....
○ ....
○ ....
○ ....

Special Reminders

○ ....
○ ....
○ ....
○ ....
○ ....
○ ....
○ ....

Week 32

Monday

Tuesday

Wednesday

Thursday

Friday

Saturday

Sunday

Places to Go

- ○
- ○
- ○
- ○
- ○
- ○

People to See

- ○
- ○
- ○
- ○
- ○
- ○

Things to Do

- ○
- ○
- ○
- ○
- ○
- ○
- ○
- ○
- ○
- ○
- ○
- ○
- ○

Special Reminders

- ○
- ○
- ○
- ○
- ○
- ○
- ○

Week 33

nday

esday

ednesday

hursday

riday

Saturday

Sunday

Places to Go

○
○
○
○
○
○

People to See

○
○
○
○
○
○

Things to Do

○
○
○
○
○
○
○
○
○
○
○
○
○

Special Reminders

○
○
○
○
○
○
○

Week 34

Monday

Tuesday

Wednesday

Thursday

Friday

Saturday

Sunday

Places to Go

- ○
- ○
- ○
- ○
- ○
- ○

People to See

- ○
- ○
- ○
- ○
- ○
- ○

Things to Do

- ○
- ○
- ○
- ○
- ○
- ○
- ○
- ○
- ○
- ○
- ○
- ○
- ○

Special Reminders

- ○
- ○
- ○
- ○
- ○
- ○
- ○

Week 35

nday

esday

ednesday

hursday

riday

Saturday

Sunday

Places to Go

- ○
- ○
- ○
- ○
- ○
- ○

People to See

- ○
- ○
- ○
- ○
- ○
- ○

Things to Do

- ○
- ○
- ○
- ○
- ○
- ○
- ○
- ○
- ○
- ○
- ○
- ○
- ○

Special Reminders

- ○
- ○
- ○
- ○
- ○
- ○
- ○

Week 36

Monday

Tuesday

Wednesday

Thursday

Friday

Saturday

Sunday

Places to Go

- ○
- ○
- ○
- ○
- ○
- ○

People to See

- ○
- ○
- ○
- ○
- ○
- ○

Things to Do

- ○
- ○
- ○
- ○
- ○
- ○
- ○
- ○
- ○
- ○
- ○
- ○
- ○

Special Reminders

- ○
- ○
- ○
- ○
- ○
- ○
- ○

Week 37

nday

esday

ednesday

hursday

riday

Saturday

Sunday

Places to Go

- ◯
- ◯
- ◯
- ◯
- ◯
- ◯

People to See

- ◯
- ◯
- ◯
- ◯
- ◯
- ◯

Things to Do

- ◯
- ◯
- ◯
- ◯
- ◯
- ◯
- ◯
- ◯
- ◯
- ◯
- ◯
- ◯
- ◯

Special Reminders

- ◯
- ◯
- ◯
- ◯
- ◯
- ◯
- ◯

Week 38

Monday

Tuesday

Wednesday

Thursday

Friday

Saturday

Sunday

Places to Go

- ○
- ○
- ○
- ○
- ○
- ○

People to See

- ○
- ○
- ○
- ○
- ○
- ○

Things to Do

- ○
- ○
- ○
- ○
- ○
- ○
- ○
- ○
- ○
- ○
- ○
- ○

Special Reminders

- ○
- ○
- ○
- ○
- ○
- ○
- ○

Week 39

Monday

Tuesday

Wednesday

Thursday

Friday

Saturday

Sunday

Places to Go

- ○
- ○
- ○
- ○
- ○
- ○

People to See

- ○
- ○
- ○
- ○
- ○
- ○

Things to Do

- ○
- ○
- ○
- ○
- ○
- ○
- ○
- ○
- ○
- ○
- ○
- ○
- ○

Special Reminders

- ○
- ○
- ○
- ○
- ○
- ○
- ○

Week 40

Monday

Tuesday

Wednesday

Thursday

Friday

Saturday

Sunday

Places to Go

○
○
○
○
○
○
○

People to See

○
○
○
○
○

Things to Do

○
○
○
○
○
○
○
○
○
○
○
○

Special Reminders

○
○
○
○
○
○

Week 41

nday

esday

ednesday

ursday

iday

aturday

unday

Places to Go

○
○
○
○
○
○

People to See

○
○
○
○
○
○

Things to Do

○
○
○
○
○
○
○
○
○
○
○
○

Special Reminders

○
○
○
○
○
○
○

Week 42

Monday

Tuesday

Wednesday

Thursday

Friday

Saturday

Sunday

Places to Go

People to See

Things to Do

Special Reminders

Week 43

nday

sday

dnesday

ursday

iday

aturday

unday

Places to Go

- ○
- ○
- ○
- ○
- ○
- ○

People to See

- ○
- ○
- ○
- ○
- ○
- ○

Things to Do

- ○
- ○
- ○
- ○
- ○
- ○
- ○
- ○
- ○
- ○
- ○
- ○
- ○

Special Reminders

- ○
- ○
- ○
- ○
- ○
- ○
- ○

Week 44

Monday

Tuesday

Wednesday

Thursday

Friday

Saturday

Sunday

Places to Go

People to See

Things to Do

Special Reminders

Week 45

Monday

Tuesday

Wednesday

Thursday

Friday

Saturday

Sunday

Places to Go
- ○
- ○
- ○
- ○
- ○
- ○

People to See
- ○
- ○
- ○
- ○
- ○
- ○

Things to Do
- ○
- ○
- ○
- ○
- ○
- ○
- ○
- ○
- ○
- ○
- ○
- ○
- ○

Special Reminders
- ○
- ○
- ○
- ○
- ○
- ○
- ○

Week 46

Monday

Tuesday

Wednesday

Thursday

Friday

Saturday

Sunday

Places to Go

People to See

Things to Do

Special Reminders

Week 47

Monday

Tuesday

Wednesday

Thursday

Friday

Saturday

Sunday

Places to Go

- ○
- ○
- ○
- ○
- ○
- ○

People to See

- ○
- ○
- ○
- ○
- ○
- ○

Things to Do

- ○
- ○
- ○
- ○
- ○
- ○
- ○
- ○
- ○
- ○
- ○
- ○
- ○

Special Reminders

- ○
- ○
- ○
- ○
- ○
- ○
- ○

Week 48

Monday

Tuesday

Wednesday

Thursday

Friday

Saturday

Sunday

Places to Go

○
○
○
○
○
○

People to See

○
○
○
○
○

Things to Do

○
○
○
○
○
○
○
○
○
○
○
○

Special Reminders

○
○
○
○
○
○

Week 49

nday

esday

ednesday

ursday

iday

aturday

unday

Places to Go

- ○
- ○
- ○
- ○
- ○
- ○

People to See

- ○
- ○
- ○
- ○
- ○
- ○

Things to Do

- ○
- ○
- ○
- ○
- ○
- ○
- ○
- ○
- ○
- ○
- ○
- ○
- ○

Special Reminders

- ○
- ○
- ○
- ○
- ○
- ○

Week 50

Monday

Tuesday

Wednesday

Thursday

Friday

Saturday

Sunday

Places to Go

People to See

Things to Do

Special Reminders

Week 51

Monday

Tuesday

Wednesday

Thursday

Friday

Saturday

Sunday

Places to Go

- ○
- ○
- ○
- ○
- ○
- ○

People to See

- ○
- ○
- ○
- ○
- ○
- ○

Things to Do

- ○
- ○
- ○
- ○
- ○
- ○
- ○
- ○
- ○
- ○
- ○
- ○

Special Reminders

- ○
- ○
- ○
- ○
- ○
- ○
- ○

Week 52

Monday

Tuesday

Wednesday

Thursday

Friday

Saturday

Sunday

Places to Go

People to See

Things to Do

Special Reminders

Week 53

nday

esday

ednesday

ursday

iday

aturday

unday

Places to Go

○
○
○
○
○
○

People to See

○
○
○
○
○
○

Things to Do

○
○
○
○
○
○
○
○
○
○
○
○
○
○

Special Reminders

○
○
○
○
○
○
○

My Personal Goals

This format will help you clarify your long-term goals. Be specific when listing goals, include at least 3 actions needed in order to achieve your goals, and don't forget a due date to ensure you take action. Keep this list in a place where you will see it each day; it will really help you stay focused on what's most important to you!

MY GOALS	ACTION STEPS	DUE DATE

LONG TERM

1.

2.

3.

1.

2.

3.

SHORT TERM

1.

2.

3.

1.

2.

3.

NOW

1.

2.

3.

1.

2.

3.

My Personal Goals

This format will help you clarify your long-term goals. Be specific when listing goals, include at least 3 actions needed in order to achieve your goals, and don't forget a due date to ensure you take action. Keep this list in a place where you will see it each day; it will really help you stay focused on what's most important to you!

MY GOALS	ACTION STEPS	DUE DATE
LONG TERM		
....	1.	....
	2.	....
	3.	....
....	1.	....
	2.	....
	3.	....
SHORT TERM		
....	1.	....
	2.	....
	3.	....
....	1.	....
	2.	....
	3.	....
NOW		
....	1.	....
	2.	....
	3.	....
....	1.	....
	2.	....
	3.	....

Vacation Planning

DATES:

LOCATION:

BUDGET:

GETTING THERE

CAR RENTAL

LODGING

WHAT TO PACK

RECOMMENDED SIGHTS/RESTAURANTS

ITINERARY

NOTES:

Packing List

ESSENTIALS

- ○ Tickets
- ○ Passports
- ○ Car Rental Info
- ○ Itinerary
- ○ Reservation Info
- ○ Cell Phone Charger
- ○ Car Cell Phone Charger
- ○ Foreign Currency
- ○ Wallet/Purse
- ○ Medications

CLOTHING

- ○ Undergarments/Socks
- ○ Shirts/Blouses
- ○ Jeans/Pants/Shorts
- ○ Sweaters
- ○ Dresses/Skirts
- ○ Jacket
- ○ Pajamas/Robe/Slippers
- ○ Shoes/Sneakers
- ○ Workout Clothing

TOILETRIES

- ○ Shampoo/Conditioner
- ○ Cleansers/Soap
- ○ Toothbrush/Toothpaste/Floss
- ○ Cosmetics
- ○ Deodorant
- ○ Lip Balm
- ○ Brush/Comb
- ○ Razor/Shaving Cream
- ○ Contact Lens Solution

MISCELLANEOUS

- ○ Jewelry/Watch
- ○ Hairdryer
- ○ Camera/Video Camera
- ○ Memory Cards
- ○ Glasses/Sunglasses
- ○ Travel Guidebooks
- ○ Travel Journal
- ○ Books/Magazines
- ○ First Aid Kit
- ○ Antibacterial Wipes/Lotion
- ○ Stain Removal Wipes

FOR THE KIDS

- ○ Stroller
- ○ Diapers/Wipes/Changing
- ○ Pad
- ○ Diaper Bag
- ○ Food/Formula
- ○ Bottles
- ○ Sippy Cups
- ○ Utensils
- ○ Bibs
- ○ Medicines
- ○ Toys/Games
- ○ Stuffed Animal
- ○ Blanket
- ○ Books
- ○ Activity Books
- ○ Handheld Games
- ○
- ○
- ○
- ○
- ○

SKI ESSENTIALS

- ○ Waterproof Ski Jacket/Pants
- ○ Long Underwear
- ○ Skis/Boots/Poles
- ○ Ski Helmet
- ○ Goggles
- ○ Ski Gloves
- ○ Neck Warmer
- ○ Hat/Headband
- ○ Ski Socks
- ○ Hand/Foot Warmers
- ○ Turtlenecks/Extra Sweaters
- ○ Snow Boots
- ○ Ski Bag

BEACH ESSENTIALS

- ○ Swimsuit/Cover Up
- ○ Sunscreen/After-Sun Lotion
- ○ Beach Towels
- ○ Beach Chairs
- ○ Beach Umbrella
- ○ Goggles
- ○ Beach/Pool Toys
- ○ Sunhat
- ○ Sandals
- ○ Beach Bag

OTHER

- ○
- ○
- ○
- ○
- ○

Websites & Passwords

WEBSITE	USERNAME	PASSWORD

Websites & Passwords

WEBSITE	USERNAME	PASSWORD

Websites & Passwords

WEBSITE	USERNAME	PASSWORD

Websites & Passwords

WEBSITE	USERNAME	PASSWORD

Notes

Notes

Notes

Notes

Notes

Notes

Notes

Party Planning

DETAILS:

MENU

BEVERAGES

GUEST NAME

RSVP Y/N

Party Planning

DETAILS:

MENU

_____
_____
_____
_____
_____
_____
_____

BEVERAGES

_____
_____
_____
_____
_____
_____
_____

GUEST NAME

_____
_____
_____
_____
_____
_____
_____
_____
_____
_____
_____
_____
_____
_____

RSVP Y/N

_____
_____
_____
_____
_____
_____
_____
_____
_____
_____
_____
_____
_____
_____

Party Planning

DETAILS:

MENU

BEVERAGES

GUEST NAME

RSVP Y/N

Party Planning

DETAILS:

MENU

BEVERAGES

GUEST NAME

RSVP Y/N

Christmas Day Planner

GUEST NAME	# OF ADULTS	# OF KIDS	FOOD ITEM TO BRING
TOTAL # OF GUESTS			

GROCERIES

ETIZERS: _____

'REES: _____

ES: _____

SSERTS: _____

VERAGES: _____

Grocery List

FRUITS
Apples
Bananas
Oranges
Lemons
Berries
Grapes
Melons

VEGETABLES
Lettuce
Spinach
Carrots
Onions
Garlic
Tomatoes
Cucumbers
Squash
Potatoes
Broccoli

MEAT
Beef
Chicken
Turkey
Fish
Seafood
Pork
Sausage
Hot Dogs
Hamburgers
Cold Cuts

DAIRY
Milk
Juice
Cheese
Butter
Eggs
Tortillas
Yogurt
Whipped Cream

PACKAGED
Chips
Cookies
Crackers
Popcorn
Pretzels
Nuts
Candy
Dips/Salsa
Fruit Cups
Energy Bars

BREADS
White
Wheat
Fresh Baked
Bagels
Muffins
English Muffins
Pita
Rolls
Donuts/Pastries

GRAINS
Pasta
Rice
Couscous
Dried Beans
Stuffing
Bread Crumbs

BREAKFAST FOOD
Oatmeal
Pancake Mix
Granola
Cereal Bars
Syrup
Cereals

BAKING GOODS
Baking Mixes
Flours
Sugars

CANNED
Soup
Broth
Tomatoes
Pasta Sauce
Beans
Tuna
Fruits
Vegetables

BEVERAGES
Soda
Beer/Wine
Energy Drinks
Juice
Water

MISCELLANEOUS
Ketchup
Mayonnaise
Salad Dressing
Peanut Butter
Jelly
Coffee
Tea
Oils
Vinegar
Salt
Pepper
Spices

FROZEN
Ice Cream
Waffles
Pizza
Fries
Bread
Meals
Snacks
Juice
Vegetables

HOUSEHOLD GOODS
Cleaning Products
Dish Liquid
Hand Soap
All-purpose
Bathroom
Floor/Carpet
Wood/Furniture
Glass/Window
Sponges
Trash Bags
Air Freshener
Hand Sanitizer
Miscellaneous

LAUNDRY
Detergent
Fabric Softener
Bleach
Starch
Stain Remover

PAPER PRODUCTS
Napkins
Paper Towels
Facial Tissue
Bathroom Tissue
Paper Plates
Paper Cups

MISC. HOUSEHOLD
Lunch Bags
Storage Bags
Storage Containers
Batteries
Coffee Filters

OTHER

Grocery List

UITS
- les
- anas
- anges
- nons
- ries
- apes
- lons

EGETABLES
- ttuce
- inach
- arrots
- nions
- arlic
- omatoes
- ucumbers
- quash
- otatoes
- roccoli

MEAT
- eef
- hicken
- urkey
- ish
- eafood
- ork
- ausage
- Hot Dogs
- Hamburgers
- Cold Cuts

DAIRY
- Milk
- Juice
- Cheese
- Butter
- Eggs
- Tortillas
- Yogurt
- Whipped Cream

PACKAGED
- Chips
- Cookies
- Crackers
- Popcorn
- Pretzels
- Nuts
- Candy
- Dips/Salsa
- Fruit Cups
- Energy Bars

BREADS
- White
- Wheat
- Fresh Baked
- Bagels
- Muffins
- English Muffins
- Pita
- Rolls
- Donuts/Pastries

GRAINS
- Pasta
- Rice
- Couscous
- Dried Beans
- Stuffing
- Bread Crumbs

BREAKFAST FOOD
- Oatmeal
- Pancake Mix
- Granola
- Cereal Bars
- Syrup
- Cereals

BAKING GOODS
- Baking Mixes
- Flours
- Sugars

CANNED
- Soup
- Broth
- Tomatoes
- Pasta Sauce
- Beans
- Tuna
- Fruits
- Vegetables

BEVERAGES
- Soda
- Beer/Wine
- Energy Drinks
- Juice
- Water

MISCELLANEOUS
- Ketchup
- Mayonnaise
- Salad Dressing
- Peanut Butter
- Jelly
- Coffee
- Tea
- Oils
- Vinegar
- Salt
- Pepper
- Spices

FROZEN
- Ice Cream
- Waffles
- Pizza
- Fries
- Bread
- Meals
- Snacks
- Juice
- Vegetables

HOUSEHOLD GOODS
- Cleaning Products
- Dish Liquid
- Hand Soap
- All-purpose
- Bathroom
- Floor/Carpet
- Wood/Furniture
- Glass/Window
- Sponges
- Trash Bags
- Air Freshener
- Hand Sanitizer
- Miscellaneous

LAUNDRY
- Detergent
- Fabric Softener
- Bleach
- Starch
- Stain Remover

PAPER PRODUCTS
- Napkins
- Paper Towels
- Facial Tissue
- Bathroom Tissue
- Paper Plates
- Paper Cups

MISC. HOUSEHOLD
- Lunch Bags
- Storage Bags
- Storage Containers
- Batteries
- Coffee Filters

OTHER

Grocery List

FRUITS
Apples
Bananas
Oranges
Lemons
Berries
Grapes
Melons

VEGETABLES
Lettuce
Spinach
Carrots
Onions
Garlic
Tomatoes
Cucumbers
Squash
Potatoes
Broccoli

MEAT
Beef
Chicken
Turkey
Fish
Seafood
Pork
Sausage
Hot Dogs
Hamburgers
Cold Cuts

DAIRY
Milk
Juice
Cheese
Butter
Eggs
Tortillas
Yogurt
Whipped Cream

PACKAGED
Chips
Cookies
Crackers
Popcorn
Pretzels
Nuts
Candy
Dips/Salsa
Fruit Cups
Energy Bars

BREADS
White
Wheat
Fresh Baked
Bagels
Muffins
English Muffins
Pita
Rolls
Donuts/Pastries

GRAINS
Pasta
Rice
Couscous
Dried Beans
Stuffing
Bread Crumbs

BREAKFAST FOOD
Oatmeal
Pancake Mix
Granola
Cereal Bars
Syrup
Cereals

BAKING GOODS
Baking Mixes
Flours
Sugars

CANNED
Soup
Broth
Tomatoes
Pasta Sauce
Beans
Tuna
Fruits
Vegetables

BEVERAGES
Soda
Beer/Wine
Energy Drinks
Juice
Water

MISCELLANEOUS
Ketchup
Mayonnaise
Salad Dressing
Peanut Butter
Jelly
Coffee
Tea
Oils
Vinegar
Salt
Pepper
Spices

FROZEN
Ice Cream
Waffles
Pizza
Fries
Bread
Meals
Snacks
Juice
Vegetables

HOUSEHOLD GOODS
Cleaning Products
Dish Liquid
Hand Soap
All-purpose
Bathroom
Floor/Carpet
Wood/Furniture
Glass/Window
Sponges
Trash Bags
Air Freshener
Hand Sanitizer
Miscellaneous

LAUNDRY
Detergent
Fabric Softener
Bleach
Starch
Stain Remover

PAPER PRODUCTS
Napkins
Paper Towels
Facial Tissue
Bathroom Tissue
Paper Plates
Paper Cups

MISC. HOUSEHOLD
Lunch Bags
Storage Bags
Storage Containers
Batteries
Coffee Filters

OTHER

Grocery List

FRUITS
- ples
- anas
- anges
- nons
- ries
- apes
- elons

VEGETABLES
- ttuce
- inach
- rrots
- nions
- arlic
- matoes
- ucumbers
- quash
- tatoes
- occoli

MEAT
- eef
- hicken
- urkey
- ish
- eafood
- ork
- ausage
- lot Dogs
- lamburgers
- old Cuts

DAIRY
- Milk
- uice
- Cheese
- Butter
- Eggs
- Tortillas
- Yogurt
- Whipped Cream

PACKAGED
- Chips
- Cookies
- Crackers
- Popcorn
- Pretzels
- Nuts
- Candy
- Dips/Salsa
- Fruit Cups
- Energy Bars

BREADS
- White
- Wheat
- Fresh Baked
- Bagels
- Muffins
- English Muffins
- Pita
- Rolls
- Donuts/Pastries

GRAINS
- Pasta
- Rice
- Couscous
- Dried Beans
- Stuffing
- Bread Crumbs

BREAKFAST FOOD
- Oatmeal
- Pancake Mix
- Granola
- Cereal Bars
- Syrup
- Cereals

BAKING GOODS
- Baking Mixes
- Flours
- Sugars

CANNED
- Soup
- Broth
- Tomatoes
- Pasta Sauce
- Beans
- Tuna
- Fruits
- Vegetables

BEVERAGES
- Soda
- Beer/Wine
- Energy Drinks
- Juice
- Water

MISCELLANEOUS
- Ketchup
- Mayonnaise
- Salad Dressing
- Peanut Butter
- Jelly
- Coffee
- Tea
- Oils
- Vinegar
- Salt
- Pepper
- Spices

FROZEN
- Ice Cream
- Waffles
- Pizza
- Fries
- Bread
- Meals
- Snacks
- Juice
- Vegetables

HOUSEHOLD GOODS
- Cleaning Products
- Dish Liquid
- Hand Soap
- All-purpose
- Bathroom
- Floor/Carpet
- Wood/Furniture
- Glass/Window
- Sponges
- Trash Bags
- Air Freshener
- Hand Sanitizer
- Miscellaneous

LAUNDRY
- Detergent
- Fabric Softener
- Bleach
- Starch
- Stain Remover

PAPER PRODUCTS
- Napkins
- Paper Towels
- Facial Tissue
- Bathroom Tissue
- Paper Plates
- Paper Cups

MISC. HOUSEHOLD
- Lunch Bags
- Storage Bags
- Storage Containers
- Batteries
- Coffee Filters

OTHER

2020

January
Su	Mo	Tu	We	Th	Fr	Sa
			1	2	3	4
5	6	7	8	9	10	11
12	13	14	15	16	17	18
19	20	21	22	23	24	25
26	27	28	29	30	31	

2◐ 10○ 17◑ 24●

February
Su	Mo	Tu	We	Th	Fr	Sa
						1
2	3	4	5	6	7	8
9	10	11	12	13	14	15
16	17	18	19	20	21	22
23	24	25	26	27	28	29

1◐ 9○ 15◑ 23●

March
Su	Mo	Tu	We	Th	Fr	Sa
1	2	3	4	5	6	7
8	9	10	11	12	13	14
15	16	17	18	19	20	21
22	23	24	25	26	27	28
29	30	31				

2◐ 9○ 16◑ 24●

April
Su	Mo	Tu	We	Th	Fr	Sa
			1	2	3	4
5	6	7	8	9	10	11
12	13	14	15	16	17	18
19	20	21	22	23	24	25
26	27	28	29	30		

1◐ 7○ 14◑ 22● 30◐

May
Su	Mo	Tu	We	Th	Fr	Sa
					1	2
3	4	5	6	7	8	9
10	11	12	13	14	15	16
17	18	19	20	21	22	23
24	25	26	27	28	29	30
31						

7○ 14◑ 22● 29◐

June
Su	Mo	Tu	We	Th	Fr	Sa
	1	2	3	4	5	6
7	8	9	10	11	12	13
14	15	16	17	18	19	20
21	22	23	24	25	26	27
28	29	30				

5○ 13◑ 21● 28◐

July
Su	Mo	Tu	We	Th	Fr	Sa
			1	2	3	4
5	6	7	8	9	10	11
12	13	14	15	16	17	18
19	20	21	22	23	24	25
26	27	28	29	30	31	

5○ 12◑ 20● 27◐

August
Su	Mo	Tu	We	Th	Fr	Sa
						1
2	3	4	5	6	7	8
9	10	11	12	13	14	15
16	17	18	19	20	21	22
23	24	25	26	27	28	29
30	31					

3○ 11◑ 18● 25◐

September
Su	Mo	Tu	We	Th	Fr	Sa
		1	2	3	4	5
6	7	8	9	10	11	12
13	14	15	16	17	18	19
20	21	22	23	24	25	26
27	28	29	30			

2○ 10◑ 17● 23◐

October
Su	Mo	Tu	We	Th	Fr	Sa
				1	2	3
4	5	6	7	8	9	10
11	12	13	14	15	16	17
18	19	20	21	22	23	24
25	26	27	28	29	30	31

1○ 9◑ 16● 23◐ 31○

November
Su	Mo	Tu	We	Th	Fr	Sa
1	2	3	4	5	6	7
8	9	10	11	12	13	14
15	16	17	18	19	20	21
22	23	24	25	26	27	28
29	30					

8◑ 15● 21◐ 30○

December
Su	Mo	Tu	We	Th	Fr	Sa
		1	2	3	4	5
6	7	8	9	10	11	12
13	14	15	16	17	18	19
20	21	22	23	24	25	26
27	28	29	30	31		

7◑ 14● 21◐ 29○

2021

January
Su	Mo	Tu	We	Th	Fr	Sa
					1	2
3	4	5	6	7	8	9
10	11	12	13	14	15	16
17	18	19	20	21	22	23
24	25	26	27	28	29	30
31						

6◑ 13● 20◐ 28○

February
Su	Mo	Tu	We	Th	Fr	Sa
	1	2	3	4	5	6
7	8	9	10	11	12	13
14	15	16	17	18	19	20
21	22	23	24	25	26	27
28						

4◑ 11● 19◐ 27○

March
Su	Mo	Tu	We	Th
	1	2	3	4
7	8	9	10	11
14	15	16	17	18
21	22	23	24	25
28	29	30	31	

5◑ 13● 21◐ 2

April
Su	Mo	Tu	We	Th	Fr	Sa
				1	2	3
4	5	6	7	8	9	10
11	12	13	14	15	16	17
18	19	20	21	22	23	24
25	26	27	28	29	30	

4◑ 11● 20◐ 26○

May
Su	Mo	Tu	We	Th	Fr	Sa
						1
2	3	4	5	6	7	8
9	10	11	12	13	14	15
16	17	18	19	20	21	22
23	24	25	26	27	28	29
30	31					

3◑ 11● 19◐ 26○

June
Su	Mo	Tu	We	Th
		1	2	3
6	7	8	9	10
13	14	15	16	17
20	21	22	23	24
27	28	29	30	

2◑ 10● 17◐ 2

July
Su	Mo	Tu	We	Th	Fr	Sa
				1	2	3
4	5	6	7	8	9	10
11	12	13	14	15	16	17
18	19	20	21	22	23	24
25	26	27	28	29	30	31

1◑ 9● 17◐ 23○ 31◑

August
Su	Mo	Tu	We	Th	Fr	Sa
1	2	3	4	5	6	7
8	9	10	11	12	13	14
15	16	17	18	19	20	21
22	23	24	25	26	27	28
29	30	31				

8● 15◐ 22○ 30◑

Septembe
Su	Mo	Tu	We	Th
			1	2
5	6	7	8	9
12	13	14	15	16
19	20	21	22	23
26	27	28	29	30

6● 13◐ 20○ 2

October
Su	Mo	Tu	We	Th	Fr	Sa
					1	2
3	4	5	6	7	8	9
10	11	12	13	14	15	16
17	18	19	20	21	22	23
24	25	26	27	28	29	30
31						

6● 12◐ 20○ 28◑

November
Su	Mo	Tu	We	Th	Fr	Sa
	1	2	3	4	5	6
7	8	9	10	11	12	13
14	15	16	17	18	19	20
21	22	23	24	25	26	27
28	29	30				

4● 11◐ 19○ 27◑

December
Su	Mo	Tu	We	Th
			1	2
5	6	7	8	9
12	13	14	15	16
19	20	21	22	23
26	27	28	29	30

4● 10◐ 18○ 2

2022

January
Su	Mo	Tu	We	Th	Fr	Sa
						1
2	3	4	5	6	7	8
9	10	11	12	13	14	15
16	17	18	19	20	21	22
23	24	25	26	27	28	29
30	31					

2● 9◐ 17○ 25◑

February
Su	Mo	Tu	We	Th	Fr	Sa
		1	2	3	4	5
6	7	8	9	10	11	12
13	14	15	16	17	18	19
20	21	22	23	24	25	26
27	28					

1● 8◐ 16○ 23◑

March
Su	Mo	Tu	We	Th	Fr	Sa
		1	2	3	4	5
6	7	8	9	10	11	12
13	14	15	16	17	18	19
20	21	22	23	24	25	26
27	28	29	30	31		

2● 10◐ 18○ 25◑

April
Su	Mo	Tu	We	Th	Fr	Sa
					1	2
3	4	5	6	7	8	9
10	11	12	13	14	15	16
17	18	19	20	21	22	23
24	25	26	27	28	29	30

1● 9◐ 16○ 23◑ 30●

May
Su	Mo	Tu	We	Th	Fr	Sa
1	2	3	4	5	6	7
8	9	10	11	12	13	14
15	16	17	18	19	20	21
22	23	24	25	26	27	28
29	30	31				

8◐ 16○ 22◑ 30●

June
Su	Mo	Tu	We	Th	Fr	Sa
			1	2	3	4
5	6	7	8	9	10	11
12	13	14	15	16	17	18
19	20	21	22	23	24	25
26	27	28	29	30		

7◐ 14○ 20◑ 28●

July
Su	Mo	Tu	We	Th	Fr	Sa
					1	2
3	4	5	6	7	8	9
10	11	12	13	14	15	16
17	18	19	20	21	22	23
24	25	26	27	28	29	30
31						

6◐ 13○ 20◑ 28●

August
Su	Mo	Tu	We	Th	Fr	Sa
	1	2	3	4	5	6
7	8	9	10	11	12	13
14	15	16	17	18	19	20
21	22	23	24	25	26	27
28	29	30	31			

5◐ 11○ 19◑ 27●

September
Su	Mo	Tu	We	Th	Fr	Sa
				1	2	3
4	5	6	7	8	9	10
11	12	13	14	15	16	17
18	19	20	21	22	23	24
25	26	27	28	29	30	

3◐ 10○ 17◑ 25●

October
Su	Mo	Tu	We	Th	Fr	Sa
						1
2	3	4	5	6	7	8
9	10	11	12	13	14	15
16	17	18	19	20	21	22
23	24	25	26	27	28	29
30	31					

2◐ 9○ 17◑ 25●

November
Su	Mo	Tu	We	Th	Fr	Sa
		1	2	3	4	5
6	7	8	9	10	11	12
13	14	15	16	17	18	19
20	21	22	23	24	25	26
27	28	29	30			

1◐ 8○ 16◑ 23● 30◐

December
Su	Mo	Tu	We	Th	Fr	Sa
				1	2	3
4	5	6	7	8	9	10
11	12	13	14	15	16	17
18	19	20	21	22	23	24
25	26	27	28	29	30	31

7○ 16◑ 23● 29◐

2023

January
Su	Mo	Tu	We	Th	Fr	Sa
1	2	3	4	5	6	7
8	9	10	11	12	13	14
15	16	17	18	19	20	21
22	23	24	25	26	27	28
29	30	31				

6○ 14◑ 21● 28◐

February
Su	Mo	Tu	We	Th	Fr	Sa
			1	2	3	4
5	6	7	8	9	10	11
12	13	14	15	16	17	18
19	20	21	22	23	24	25
26	27	28				

5○ 13◑ 20● 27◐

March
Su	Mo	Tu	We	Th
			1	2
5	6	7	8	9
12	13	14	15	16
19	20	21	22	23
26	27	28	29	30

7○ 14◑ 21● 2

April
Su	Mo	Tu	We	Th	Fr	Sa
						1
2	3	4	5	6	7	8
9	10	11	12	13	14	15
16	17	18	19	20	21	22
23	24	25	26	27	28	29
30						

6○ 13◑ 20● 27◐

May
Su	Mo	Tu	We	Th	Fr	Sa
	1	2	3	4	5	6
7	8	9	10	11	12	13
14	15	16	17	18	19	20
21	22	23	24	25	26	27
28	29	30	31			

5○ 12◑ 19● 27◐

June
Su	Mo	Tu	We	Th
				1
4	5	6	7	8
11	12	13	14	15
18	19	20	21	22
25	26	27	28	29

3○ 10◑ 18● 2

July
Su	Mo	Tu	We	Th	Fr	Sa
						1
2	3	4	5	6	7	8
9	10	11	12	13	14	15
16	17	18	19	20	21	22
23	24	25	26	27	28	29
30	31					

3○ 9◑ 17● 25◐

August
Su	Mo	Tu	We	Th	Fr	Sa
		1	2	3	4	5
6	7	8	9	10	11	12
13	14	15	16	17	18	19
20	21	22	23	24	25	26
27	28	29	30	31		

1○ 8◑ 16● 24◐ 30○

September
Su	Mo	Tu	We	Th
3	4	5	6	7
10	11	12	13	14
17	18	19	20	21
24	25	26	27	28

6◑ 14● 22◐

October
Su	Mo	Tu	We	Th	Fr	Sa
1	2	3	4	5	6	7
8	9	10	11	12	13	14
15	16	17	18	19	20	21
22	23	24	25	26	27	28
29	30	31				

6◑ 14● 21◐ 28○

November
Su	Mo	Tu	We	Th	Fr	Sa
			1	2	3	4
5	6	7	8	9	10	11
12	13	14	15	16	17	18
19	20	21	22	23	24	25
26	27	28	29	30		

5◑ 13● 20◐ 27○

December
Su	Mo	Tu	We	Th
3	4	5	6	7
10	11	12	13	14
17	18	19	20	21
24	25	26	27	28
31				

5◑ 12● 19◐ 2

Manufactured by Amazon.ca
Bolton, ON

25448655R00061